UNLOCKING FINANCIAL SUCCESS

Strategies For Wealth Building

JOHN DOLLAR

Copyright © 2024

by

John dollar

Table of Contents

INTRODUCTION

In the bustling city of Eldoria, where the skyline was decorated with towering skyscrapers and the streets hummed with the rhythm of ambition, lived young entrepreneur Alex Mercer. Born into a middle-class family, Alex always dreamed of unlocking the door to financial success and creating a legacy that would resonate for generations to come.

Growing up, Alex showed an incredible aptitude for technology. In early high school, while his peers were immersed in typical teenage activities, Alex spent his evenings immersed in coding and software development. His passion for innovation led him to create a revolutionary app that caught the attention of investors. However, despite the initial success, the road to financial prosperity was fraught with problems.

Undeterred, Alex sought guidance from seasoned mentors who had walked similar paths. One such mentor, a shrewd business mogul named Evelyn Hart, recognized the spark in Alex's eyes and took him under her wing. Together, they embarked on a journey that redefined the meaning of financial success.

Evelyn imparted invaluable lessons about resilience, strategic thinking, and the importance of building a strong foundation. Under her guidance, Alex honed his business talent and learned not only to navigate the volatile market, but also to anticipate trends and take advantage of emerging opportunities.

As their collaboration flourished, Alex and Evelyn explored new ventures and diversified their portfolios to mitigate risk. They have delved into industries that align with Alex's technology expertise, from artificial intelligence to renewable energy. With each successful endeavor, the duo amassed both wealth and influence.

However, the road to financial success was not without its share of setbacks. The duo faced tough competition, encountered unpredictable market fluctuations and weathered the storm of the economic downturn. Yet each obstacle became a springboard, driving them forward with newfound determination.

In the midst of their triumphs, Alex stayed grounded and never forgot the struggles that shaped him. His philanthropic endeavors became a testament to his belief in giving back to the community. From funding educational initiatives to supporting local businesses, Alex has ensured that the ripples of his success reach far beyond the walls of his boardroom.

One pivotal moment in their journey came when they came across a breakthrough technology that had the potential to revolutionize the healthcare industry. Driven by a desire to make a meaningful impact, Alex envisioned a future where this innovation could save lives and improve the well-being of millions.

The duo poured resources into research and development and assembled a team of brilliant minds determined to bring their vision to life. As the project progressed, they faced ethical dilemmas and regulatory hurdles. Yet their unwavering commitment to the greater good fueled their determination.

The breakthrough came when they successfully launched a medical device that could diagnose diseases with unprecedented speed and accuracy. The innovation garnered international acclaim and brought them not only financial success, but also recognition for their commitment to developing healthcare.

In the midst of their success, Alex reflected on the transformative power of financial success. It wasn't just about accumulating wealth, it was about creating positive change and leaving a lasting legacy. He realized that the journey was as important as the destination.

As the years passed, Alex and Evelyn became pioneers in their fields. Their story has become a source of inspiration for budding entrepreneurs around the world. They have established scholarship programs, mentoring initiatives and incubators to nurture the next generation of innovators.

But with success came the responsibility of navigating the complexities of wealth. Alex embraced his role as a steward of prosperity and prioritized sustainable practices and ethical business conduct. He understood that true financial success goes beyond individual profit to include the well-being of society and the environment.

In the twilight of his career, Alex found fulfillment in the impact he made. The city of Eldoria, once the backdrop of his dreams, now bore the fingerprints of his efforts. The Mercer Foundation has funded countless projects, from green energy initiatives to education programs, that have shaped a future that transcends the boundaries of financial prosperity.

As Alex looked back on his journey, he realized that unlocking financial success was not just a goal, but an ongoing effort. It was about accepting challenges, learning from failures and using success as a catalyst for positive change. In the tapestry of his life, financial success was but one thread, intricately woven with resilience, vision and determination to leave the world better than he found it.

Unlocking financial success is a journey that combines individual aspirations, strategic planning and a nuanced understanding of the ever-evolving economic environment. In a world where financial stability is the desired goal, the road to prosperity requires a multifaceted approach. This introduction delves into the key elements that go into unlocking financial success, including personal finance strategies, investment wisdom, and cultivating a resilient mindset.

The basis of financial success is the art of effective budgeting and prudent money management. Building a solid foundation starts with understanding your income, expenses and savings potential. Creating a realistic budget that aligns with personal goals is similar to designing a blueprint for financial success. This involves prioritizing needs, distinguishing them from wants, and creating a sustainable balance that supports both short-term comfort and long-term wealth accumulation.

At the same time, cultivating a disciplined approach to saving is a fundamental aspect of financial success. Whether through traditional savings accounts, investment vehicles, or a combination of the two, saving is the cornerstone of building a financial safety net. It not only provides protection against unexpected expenses, but also lays the foundation for future investments that can bring significant returns.

The transition from saving to investing is a pivotal step in the pursuit of financial success. While saving preserves wealth, strategic investments have the potential to multiply it. Understanding the various investment options, from stocks and bonds to real estate and mutual funds, allows individuals to make informed decisions consistent with their risk tolerance and financial goals. Diversification, a key principle in investing, spreads risk and increases the potential for returns, contributing to long-term financial success.

In the dynamic world of finance, being informed is paramount. Financial literacy equips individuals with the knowledge to make good decisions, adapt to market trends and take advantage of opportunities. This includes keeping abreast of economic indicators, understanding the impact of global events on financial markets, and constantly improving your knowledge of investment strategies. Additionally, seeking advice from financial experts and mentors can provide valuable insights to help you navigate the complexities of the financial landscape.

However, financial success does not depend only on monetary acumen. Developing a resilient mindset is equally essential. The ability to persevere through financial challenges, bounce back from setbacks, and maintain a positive outlook in the face of uncertainty contributes significantly to long-term success. This resilience extends beyond financial decisions to include career choices, entrepreneurial endeavors, and the pursuit of lifelong learning.

Taking a proactive approach to career development is another aspect of financial success. In a rapidly evolving job market, individuals must continually upgrade their skills, seek new opportunities, and position themselves as valuable contributors to their respective industries. Career advancement often correlates with increased earning potential, providing an additional path to financial growth.

Entrepreneurship represents a unique path to financial success, offering the prospect of unlimited income potential and autonomy. Initiating and managing a successful business involves risk-taking, innovation and adaptability. Entrepreneurs manage challenges, learn from failures, and seize opportunities to build sustainable businesses that contribute not only to personal wealth, but also to the broader economic environment.

Furthermore, the concept of financial success goes beyond personal gain. Many individuals find fulfillment in contributing to social causes, philanthropy, and community development. Integrating a sense of purpose into financial endeavors adds depth to the pursuit of success and promotes a holistic approach that considers the impact of wealth on individuals and society.

Unlocking financial success is a multifaceted endeavor that combines prudent financial management, strategic investments, continuous learning, resilience, and a sense of purpose. This journey is unique to each individual and is shaped by personal aspirations, values and circumstances. By adopting the principles outlined in this introduction, individuals can embark on a path that not only leads to financial prosperity, but also enriches their lives and those around them.

Chapter 1 Foundations of Financial Success

Achieving financial success is a journey that requires a solid foundation built on key principles and practices. In this examination of the foundations of financial success, we dive into the essential elements that pave the way to prosperity. From effective budgeting to wise investing, these principles form the foundation upon which individuals can unlock the door to financial abundance.

Understanding financial goals:
Setting clear and realistic financial goals is the first step to building a foundation for success. Whether it's buying a home, saving for education, or building a nest egg for retirement, well-defined goals help guide financial decisions. Setting both short-term and long-term goals provides individuals with

guidance on how to navigate the complex landscape of personal finance.

Budgeting: the cornerstone:
At the heart of financial stability is the practice of budgeting. A budget serves as a plan for managing income and expenses and allows individuals to allocate resources wisely. It involves tracking spending habits, identifying areas for improvement and ensuring money is allocated to essentials, savings and discretionary spending. A well-constructed budget is the cornerstone of financial success.

Emergency fund: safety net :
Life is unpredictable and financial setbacks are inevitable. Building an emergency fund acts as a safety net during unforeseen circumstances such as medical emergencies or job loss. Having three to six months of living expenses set aside in a liquid and easily accessible account provides financial security and peace of mind.

Debt Management: Breaking the Chains:

Effective debt management is critical to financial success. Excessive debt can hinder progress and limit financial freedom. Ditching high-interest debt and adopting strategies like debt consolidation or refinancing can help break chains of debt and allow individuals to redirect resources toward wealth-building activities.

Investment for growth:
Investing is a powerful tool for wealth creation. While risk is inherent to investing, understanding your risk tolerance and diversifying your investments across asset classes can mitigate potential losses. Long-term investments, such as retirement accounts and diversified portfolios, help accumulate wealth over time.

Financial Literacy: Empowering Options:
Knowledge is power, especially in personal finance. Developing financial literacy is essential for making informed decisions about investments, taxes and other financial matters. Continuous learning and awareness of economic trends enables individuals to navigate the ever-evolving financial environment.

Income Streams: Building Resilience:

Relying on just one source of income can be precarious. Building multiple streams of income, such as investments, side hustles, or passive sources of income, increases financial resilience. Diversifying income streams provides a buffer against economic downturns and unexpected financial problems.

Tax planning: Maximizing returns:

Understanding the tax code and implementing effective tax planning strategies is key to maximizing returns and preserving wealth. The use of tax-advantaged accounts, the use of tax breaks and the strategic timing of financial transactions are essential components of a comprehensive tax plan.

Lifestyle Choices: Balancing Spending and Enjoyment:

Financial success is not just about accumulating wealth; it is also about achieving a balanced and fulfilling life. Making conscious lifestyle choices that align with financial goals involves finding a balance between spending on experiences and enjoying the present while saving and investing for the future.

Legacy planning: Ensuring lasting impact:
Planning for the future transcends one's life. Legacy planning involves creating a comprehensive estate plan, including wills, trusts and beneficiary designations. Ensuring distribution of assets according to wishes and minimizing tax consequences contributes to a lasting financial legacy.

Ongoing evaluation and adaptation:
The financial environment is dynamic and requires individuals to constantly adapt. Regularly evaluating financial goals, adjusting budgets, and reassessing investment strategies are critical to staying on course. Flexibility and adaptability are key qualities for those seeking lasting financial success.

The foundations of financial success are multifaceted and include budgeting, goal setting, investing, and continuous learning. By incorporating these principles into their daily financial practices, individuals can unlock the path to prosperity. Financial success is not a destination, but a journey, and building a solid foundation ensures a resilient and prosperous future.

1.1 Understanding Financial Goals

Understanding your financial goals is essential to achieving financial success. Your financial goals serve as a road map that guides you through the labyrinth of personal finance toward a secure and prosperous future. Whether it's buying a home, funding your children's education or a comfortable retirement, having well-defined financial goals is the cornerstone of financial planning.

To embark on the path to financial success, it is essential to first identify and formulate your financial goals. Start by distinguishing between short-term and long-term goals. Short-term goals might include building an emergency fund or paying off high-interest debt, while long-term goals might include saving for retirement or building a robust investment portfolio.

Once your goals are clear, it's time to quantify them. Assign specific, measurable goals and realistic time frames to each goal. This precision transforms vague aspirations into actionable steps that provide a clear picture of what needs to be achieved and when. For example, setting a goal to save $10,000 for a down payment on a house over the next two years makes that goal tangible and achievable.

Understanding your current financial situation is paramount to setting realistic goals. Do a thorough assessment of your income, expenses, assets and liabilities. This comprehensive overview provides insight into your financial health and allows you to align your goals with your current circumstances. For example, if you are struggling with significant debt, your primary goal may be to reduce debt before focusing on other goals.

Financial goals are not static; they evolve with the changes in your life. Marriage, parenthood, career progression or health issues can significantly affect your financial situation. Reassess and adjust your goals regularly to ensure they remain relevant and achievable. Flexibility is the key to adapting your financial plan to the dynamic nature of life.

Creating a budget is a crucial step to achieving your financial goals. A budget acts as a financial compass that guides your spending to match your goals. Categorize your expenses, allocate funds to each category and track your expenses regularly. This disciplined approach ensures that you allocate sufficient resources to your goals and avoid unnecessary financial detours.

Savings are the backbone of achieving financial goals. Cultivate the habit of saving by consistently putting aside a portion of your income. Establishing an emergency fund is the first line of defense against unforeseen expenses, providing a financial buffer in times of need. Once the emergency fund is built, direct your savings toward specific goals, whether it's buying a car, a dream vacation, or investing in the future.

Smart investing is another critical aspect of financial success. While savings provide stability, investments offer the potential for growth. Diversify your investment portfolio based on your risk tolerance, time horizon and financial goals.

Whether it's stocks, bonds, real estate or retirement accounts, a well-balanced portfolio can increase your wealth over time.

Regularly track and evaluate your progress toward your financial goals. Regular reviews allow you to celebrate successes, identify obstacles, and make necessary adjustments. If you are not achieving your goals, assess the reasons for this shortfall and recalibrate your strategy accordingly. Consistent tracking ensures you stay on course and make informed decisions that move you toward financial success.

Financial literacy is a powerful tool for understanding and achieving your financial goals. Educate yourself about different financial instruments, investment strategies and tax implications. A well-informed approach allows you to make sound financial decisions and optimize your resources for maximum impact.

Understanding your financial goals is a fundamental pillar for achieving financial success. Clearly define your goals, quantify them and align them with your current financial situation. Create a budget, develop the habit of saving, invest wisely and regularly evaluate your progress. Financial success is a journey, and with a well-crafted plan, disciplined execution, and adaptability, you can set yourself on the path to a secure and prosperous future.

1.2 Creating a Personal Financial Roadmap

Having a well-defined personal financial plan is essential on the road to financial success. This plan serves as a guide to help individuals navigate the complex landscape of personal finance to achieve their money goals. In this comprehensive survey, we dive into the key components of creating a robust financial plan and how they contribute to financial success.

1. Setting clear financial goals

The foundation of any effective financial plan is setting clear and achievable financial goals. These goals act as beacons, providing direction and motivation. Whether it's saving for a home, financing your education, or planning for retirement, formulating specific and measurable goals is the first step to financial success.

2. Setting a budget and managing expenses

A successful financial plan requires a careful approach to budgeting and managing expenses. Understanding where money is being spent enables informed decision-making and identification of areas of potential savings. By creating a realistic budget and tracking spending, individuals gain control over their financial resources, a critical aspect of achieving long-term financial success.

3. Emergency fund and risk management

Financial security is conditioned by the ability to weather unexpected storms. An emergency fund acts as a financial safety net that provides a cushion against unforeseen expenses or income shortfalls. Integrating risk management, such as insurance coverage, into the roadmap provides protection against potential financial setbacks and contributes to overall financial stability.

4. Debt Reduction Strategy

For many individuals, managing and reducing debt is an integral part of their financial journey. A well-structured plan includes strategies for systematically paying off high-interest debt. Prioritizing debt reduction not only improves financial health, but also frees up resources for wealth-building activities.

5. Investment Planning for Wealth Growth

Investing is a powerful tool for accumulating wealth. A comprehensive financial plan outlines personalized investment strategies in line with individual risk tolerance and financial goals. From stocks and bonds to real estate and retirement accounts, diversifying your investments contributes to steady growth of wealth over time.

6. Retirement Planning

Retirement planning is a critical part of any financial plan. Establishing retirement savings ensures financial independence during the golden years. Whether through employer-sponsored retirement accounts or personal savings, a well-thought-out retirement strategy ensures a comfortable lifestyle after employment.

7. Tax planning and optimization

Effective tax planning is a strategic aspect of financial success. Understanding the tax implications and optimizing available deductions can significantly impact disposable income. A well-informed plan includes tax-efficient strategies to minimize liabilities and maximize savings.

8. Constant learning and adaptation

The financial environment is dynamic and successful navigation requires constant learning and adaptation. A robust financial plan includes provisions for constant communication about changes in economic conditions, investment opportunities and financial strategies. This adaptability ensures that the plan remains relevant and effective over time.

9. Regular monitoring and adjustments

Creating a financial plan is not a one-time task; requires ongoing monitoring and adjustments. Life circumstances, economic conditions and personal goals evolve. Regular reassessment and adjustment of the plan ensures compliance with current reality and optimizes the chances of achieving financial success.

Unlocking financial success is a multifaceted journey that begins with creating a personalized financial plan. By setting clear goals, managing expenses, tackling debt, and strategically planning for the future through investments and retirement strategies, individuals can pave the way to financial prosperity. In addition, incorporating risk management, tax planning, continuous learning and regular adjustments increases the resilience and effectiveness of a financial plan. Ultimately, a well-crafted financial plan acts as a compass that guides individuals toward their financial aspirations and allows them to navigate the complexities of personal finance with confidence.

1.3 Importance of a Strong Financial Mindset

A strong financial mindset is the cornerstone of financial success and achieving long-term prosperity. It goes beyond just managing money; it encompasses the set of beliefs, attitudes and behaviors that shape the way individuals approach their finances. In this time of economic uncertainty and rapid change, cultivating a robust financial mindset is more important than ever.

At the heart of a strong financial mindset is the understanding that financial success is not just about making more money, but about how effectively one manages, invests and grows one's resources. This way of thinking emphasizes the importance of financial education and continuous learning. Individuals with strong financial mindsets are proactive in seeking knowledge about budgeting, investing and wealth building strategies. They realize that financial literacy is the key to making informed decisions that lead to sustainable financial success.

Additionally, a strong financial mindset involves cultivating discipline and self-control in financial matters. This includes developing the ability to distinguish between wants and needs, practicing delayed gratification, and avoiding impulsive spending. By embracing frugality and mindful spending, individuals with a strong financial mindset ensure that their resources are allocated efficiently, creating a solid foundation for building wealth.

Setting clear financial goals is another integral aspect of a strong financial mindset. Successful individuals understand the importance of defining short-term and long-term financial goals, whether it's buying a home, funding education, or a comfortable retirement. These goals serve as a road map that guides financial decisions and helps individuals focus on their financial journey. A strong financial mindset is goal-oriented, providing motivation and a sense of purpose in financial endeavors.

Risk-taking is an inherent part of financial affairs, and a robust financial mindset enables individuals to navigate risks wisely. It involves a balanced approach to risk, with the understanding that calculated risks are often necessary for financial growth. Individuals with strong financial mindsets learn to manage risk through diversification, thorough research, and a long-term perspective. This resilience to financial uncertainty is a key factor in achieving success.

When discussing a strong financial mindset, the importance of adaptability cannot be overlooked. The financial environment is dynamic and markets, regulations and economic conditions are constantly changing. People with a resilient financial mindset will embrace change and adapt their strategies accordingly. Whether it's adjusting investment portfolios, exploring new revenue streams, or implementing innovative financial technologies, adaptability is the hallmark of successful financial management.

Building and maintaining healthy financial relationships is another dimension of a strong financial mindset. It involves effective communication about financial matters with family members, business partners or financial advisors. Successful individuals understand the importance of collaboration and seek expert advice when needed. Networking and building a support system add to the overall strength of your financial mindset. Additionally, a strong financial mindset is characterized by a focus on long-term wealth building rather than short-term gains. It involves patience and perseverance in the face of challenges. Individuals with this mindset understand that building significant wealth takes time and effort. They avoid get-rich-quick schemes and instead choose sustainable, well-thought-out financial strategies.

Financial independence is a key goal for many, and a strong financial mindset is key to achieving this milestone. It allows individuals to take control of their financial destiny and reduces dependence on external factors. This independence provides a sense of security and peace of mind knowing that one has the ability to weather financial storms and make decisions in line with one's values and priorities.

The importance of a strong financial mindset in unlocking financial success cannot be overstated. It is the foundation on which sound financial decisions are made, goals are achieved and long-term prosperity is ensured. By cultivating a mindset that values financial education, discipline, goal setting, adaptability and resilience, individuals can confidently navigate the complexities of the financial world, ultimately unlocking the door to lasting financial success.

Chapter 2. Building a Strong Financial Foundation

Achieving financial success is a goal that resonates with many individuals. However, this success is not the result of chance; it requires deliberate planning, discipline and building a strong financial base. In this comprehensive guide, we'll explore the essential steps and principles involved in building a robust financial foundation that will lay the foundation for long-term financial prosperity.

1. Understanding Financial Goals and Values:

To build a solid financial foundation, it is essential to start with a clear understanding of your financial goals and values. Think about what is most important to you, both short-term and long-term. Whether it's home ownership, education, travel or retirement, aligning your financial decisions with your values provides a guiding framework.

2. Budget: The basis of financial stability:

A well-structured budget is the cornerstone of any strong financial foundation. Create a comprehensive budget that outlines your income, expenses and savings goals. Track your spending habits and identify areas where adjustments can be made. A well-maintained budget ensures that you live within your means and allocate resources wisely.

3. Emergency Fund: A Shield Against Financial Storms:

Life is unpredictable and unexpected expenses can appear at any time. Establishing an emergency fund is critical to weathering these financial storms. Aim to save three to six months of living expenses in a liquid, easily accessible account. This fund acts as a financial safety net and provides peace of mind in times of crisis.

4. Debt Management: Break Free from the Chains:

High-interest debt can significantly hinder financial progress. Prioritize paying off debts, starting with those with the highest interest rates.

Adopt a strategic debt repayment plan and consider debt consolidation for more favorable terms. The sooner you eliminate debt, the more resources you can devote to building wealth.

5. Investment for long-term growth:

Investing is a powerful tool for building wealth over time. Understand your risk tolerance, investment goals and time horizon. Diversify your investments across asset classes to mitigate risk. Consistent long-term investing allows your money to grow through compound interest, helping you achieve financial success.

6. Retirement Planning: Preparing for the Golden Years:

Building a strong financial foundation includes planning for retirement. Make regular contributions to retirement accounts such as 401(k)s or IRAs. Take advantage of employer-sponsored retirement plans and any available matching contributions. Start early to take advantage of the compounding effect and ensure a comfortable retirement lifestyle.

7. Insurance: Protecting Your Financial Future:

Adequate insurance coverage is a crucial aspect of financial planning. Whether it's health, life or property insurance, the right coverage will protect you and your loved ones from unforeseen circumstances. Regularly review and update your insurance policies to ensure they are in line with your evolving needs.

8. Continuous Education and Skills Development:

The financial environment is dynamic and staying informed is key to making informed decisions. Invest in your financial education by keeping up with economic trends, market developments and personal finance strategies. Continuously improve your skills to stay adaptable in an ever-changing financial environment.

9. Estate Planning: Passing on an Inheritance:

As part of a comprehensive financial foundation, estate planning is vital. Draft a will, establish trusts if necessary and designate beneficiaries. Proper estate planning ensures that your assets are distributed according to your wishes, minimizing legal complications for your heirs.

10. Regular Financial Controls: Adapting to Changing Circumstances:

Life is dynamic and your financial plan should adapt to changing circumstances. Conduct regular financial reviews to assess progress, reassess goals and make necessary adjustments. A flexible and adaptable financial plan is more likely to withstand unforeseen challenges.

Building a strong financial foundation is a deliberate and ongoing process that involves a combination of careful planning, disciplined execution and adaptability. By aligning your financial decisions with your values, managing your resources wisely, and investing in the future, you can unlock the door to long-term financial success. Remember, the road to financial prosperity is a marathon, not a sprint, and every step you take today contributes to a more secure and prosperous tomorrow.

2.1 Budgeting and Financial Planning

Budgeting and financial planning are essential components on the road to financial success. In a world where financial stability is often fleeting, individuals who master the art of managing their finances wisely are in a better position to achieve their goals and dreams. This contextual survey delves into the importance of budgeting and financial planning, and clarifies how these practices serve as cornerstones for building a secure financial future.

Understanding the Basics

Budget:
Budgeting is basically a plan for managing your money. It involves creating a plan that outlines your income and expenses and allows you to allocate funds to different aspects of your life, such as housing, transportation, food and discretionary expenses. A well-crafted budget serves as a financial compass, helping individuals make

informed decisions about their money and ensuring they live within their means.

Financial planning:
Financial planning, on the other hand, goes beyond the immediate framework of budgeting. It includes a holistic approach to financial management that takes into account long-term goals, investments and wealth accumulation strategies. A robust financial plan considers factors such as retirement planning, insurance, investments and tax management to provide a comprehensive framework for achieving financial success.

The nexus between budgeting and financial success

1. Building the foundations of discipline:
Budgeting brings discipline to financial habits. It requires individuals to monitor their spending, prioritize needs over wants, and make informed decisions about their financial resources. This disciplined approach lays the foundation for

financial success by encouraging responsible financial behavior.

2. Debt Management:
Budgeting is an effective tool for managing and reducing debt. By budgeting a portion of income for debt repayment, individuals can systematically eliminate outstanding balances, freeing up more resources for savings and investment. This in turn contributes to overall financial well-being.

3. Emergency Fund Creation:
A well-structured budget allows for the creation and maintenance of an emergency fund. This financial cushion provides a safety net during unexpected events, such as medical emergencies or job loss, and prevents individuals from derailing their financial progress when faced with unforeseen challenges.

4. Target Savings:
Financial planning involves setting specific financial goals, whether it's buying a home, funding education, or a comfortable retirement. Budgeting

facilitates the realization of these goals by allocating funds for each goal. By aligning budget allocations with long-term aspirations, individuals can systematically work towards their achievement.

5. Investment opportunities:

Financial planning goes hand in hand with investment strategies. Once basic budget needs are met, surplus funds can be channeled into investments. Whether it's stocks, bonds, real estate or retirement accounts, a sound financial plan guides individuals in making informed investment decisions and maximizes the potential for wealth accumulation.

6. Tax optimization:

Effective financial planning includes optimizing tax strategies. By understanding the tax implications of various financial decisions, individuals can minimize their tax liability and keep more of their hard-earned money. This essentially contributes to the overall success of their financial plan.

7. Retirement Readiness:

One of the main goals of financial planning is to ensure a comfortable retirement. Through careful budgeting and strategic financial planning, individuals can build a retirement nest egg that provides financial security and peace of mind in their later years.

Overcoming challenges in budgeting and financial planning

1. Psychological barriers:
Many individuals face psychological barriers when it comes to budgeting. Fear of facing financial reality or the perception that budgeting limits lifestyle choices can prevent the adoption of sound financial practices. Overcoming these obstacles requires a shift in mindset and an emphasis on the empowerment that comes with financial control.

2. Lack of financial literacy:
A significant obstacle to effective financial planning is the lack of financial literacy. Many people are not well informed about managing their finances, investing or understanding complex financial

instruments. Bridging this knowledge gap through education and outreach initiatives is critical to supporting informed financial decision-making.

3. Unforeseen circumstances:

Life is unpredictable and unpredictable circumstances can upset even the most careful financial plans. Building flexibility into financial strategies, such as maintaining an emergency fund and contingency plans, can mitigate the impact of unexpected events.

4. Consistency and Patience:

Financial success is a journey that requires consistency and patience. Both budgeting and financial planning require constant commitment and adjustments. It's important to remember that progress can be gradual and being able to stay the course is key to unlocking long-term financial success.

Budgeting and financial planning are an integral part of the path to financial success. Budgeting serves as an immediate, day-to-day guide that promotes discipline and responsible financial behavior. Financial planning, on the other hand, provides an overarching framework for achieving long-term goals and building wealth.

By understanding the connection between budgeting and financial success, individuals can overcome challenges, adopt prudent financial habits, and navigate the complexities of personal finance. The path to financial success is not one-size-fits-all, but with a well-crafted budget and comprehensive financial plan, individuals can unlock the door to financial security and prosperity.

2.2 Emergency Fund Strategies

In the unpredictable environment of personal finance, having a robust emergency fund is akin to building a solid foundation for a house. It provides stability, security and peace of mind, allowing individuals to weather unforeseen financial storms without compromising their long-term goals. In this examination of emergency fund strategies, we'll dive into the importance of emergency funds, the optimal ways to build and maintain them, and how this financial safety net plays a key role in unlocking overall financial success.

Financial safety net:
An emergency fund acts as a safety net to protect individuals and families from unexpected expenses such as medical emergencies, car repairs, or sudden job loss. Without this safety net, individuals may find themselves resorting to high-interest debt or depleting their savings earmarked for future goals.

Reducing stress and anxiety:
The psychological impact of financial uncertainty can be profound. An emergency fund minimizes stress and anxiety and provides a sense of security that allows individuals to make more informed financial decisions. Knowing that there is a financial buffer can lead to better overall mental well-being.

Avoiding the Debt Spiral:

When faced with unexpected expenses, individuals without an emergency fund may turn to credit cards or loans, which can lead to a cycle of debt. A contingency fund helps break this cycle by providing funds to cover unforeseen expenses and reducing reliance on borrowed money.

Building an emergency fund

Setting realistic goals:
Start by setting a realistic goal for your emergency fund. Financial experts often recommend saving three to six months for living expenses. Consider your lifestyle, job stability and any potential factors that may affect your income. Adjust the target amount accordingly.

Consistent access to savings:
Building an emergency fund is a gradual process. Set a monthly savings goal and automate transfers to your emergency fund account. Consistency is key; even small contributions can add up over time to create a substantial safety net.

Separate account for visibility:

Open a separate savings account specifically for your emergency fund. This separation helps prevent accidental spending and allows you to easily monitor the growth of your fund. Choose an account with a competitive interest rate to maximize your savings.

Unexpected and Bonuses:

Use windfalls like tax refunds or work bonuses to boost your emergency fund. While it may be tempting to allocate these funds to other financial goals, strengthening your safety net should take priority.

Maintenance and use of emergency fund

Regular Reviews:

Regularly review and reassess your emergency fund. As your life circumstances change, adjust your savings goals accordingly. An increase in the cost of living or a change in income may require a larger contingency fund.

For true emergencies only:

Discipline is key when it comes to your emergency fund. Reserve its use for true emergencies, such as medical expenses, necessary home repairs, or an unexpected job loss. Avoid dipping into your non-emergency fund to ensure it's available when you need it most.

Add after use:

If you need to tap into your emergency fund, plan to top it up quickly. Make it a priority to restore your financial safety net to optimal levels. This proactive approach ensures that your emergency fund remains a reliable resource.

The Role of Emergency Funds in Financial Success:

Protection of long-term goals:

An emergency fund is not just a financial safety net; it is a strategic tool that protects your long-term financial goals. Without such a cushion, unexpected expenses can derail plans for home ownership, education or retirement.

Increasing financial resilience:

Financial success is not just about accumulating wealth; it is also about resilience in the face of challenges. An emergency fund increases financial resilience by providing protection against unforeseen circumstances and allowing individuals to stick to their financial goals.

Decreasing dependence on credit:

For many, credit cards or loans become the default solution when faced with unexpected expenses. An emergency fund reduces reliance on credit, minimizes interest payments, and preserves financial resources for wealth-building activities rather than debt service.

In the labyrinth of personal finance, an emergency fund stands as a beacon of financial stability. Its importance goes beyond mere financial prudence; it is the cornerstone to achieving lasting financial success. By adopting sound strategies for building, maintaining, and using an emergency fund, individuals can navigate life's uncertainties with confidence and protect their dreams and aspirations. Remember, an emergency fund isn't an afterthought on the road to financial success—it's a strategic imperative.

2.3 Debt Management Strategies

In the complex environment of personal finance, effective debt management is a critical part of achieving long-term financial success. As individuals navigate the complexities of loans, credit cards and other financial obligations, taking strategic approaches to debt can pave the way to a more secure and prosperous future.

Understanding the Debt Landscape:
Before diving into specific debt management strategies, it is essential to understand the different forms of debt that individuals commonly encounter. Mortgages, student loans, credit card debt and personal loans all have their own unique terms, interest rates and repayment structures. A comprehensive understanding of these nuances is

the basis for developing a tailored debt management plan.

1. Create a detailed financial overview:

To get on the path to effective debt management, start by creating a comprehensive overview of your financial situation. A list of all outstanding debts, including their respective interest rates and minimum monthly payments. At the same time, draw up a detailed budget with an overview of your income, expenses and discretionary expenses. This snapshot serves as the basis for creating a personalized debt repayment strategy.

2. Prioritize high interest debts:

One of the basic principles of debt management is prioritizing high-interest debt. High-interest loans, usually associated with credit cards, can accumulate significant interest over time, hindering financial progress. Allocate additional funds to these debts first, while maintaining minimum payments on other obligations. This targeted approach accelerates overall debt reduction and minimizes interest costs.

3. Consolidation and refinancing:

For those juggling multiple debts with varying interest rates, debt consolidation or refinancing may be a viable option. Debt consolidation involves combining multiple loans into one payment, simplifying the repayment process. On the other hand, refinancing means replacing an existing loan with a new one, often with more favorable terms. Both strategies aim to make repayment more efficient and, in some cases, reduce overall interest payments.

4. Establish emergency savings:

Creating an emergency fund is a key part of successful debt management. A financial safety net provides protection against unforeseen expenses and reduces the likelihood of accumulating additional debt during challenging times. Aim to save three to six months of living expenses in an easily accessible account that offers peace of mind and financial stability.

5. Adopt a frugal lifestyle:

While actively managing your debt, adopting a frugal lifestyle can speed up the repayment process. Evaluate discretionary spending and identify areas where cuts are possible. Redirecting savings to pay off debt accelerates the path to financial freedom. Small sacrifices today can yield significant financial rewards in the long run.

6. Negotiation with creditors:

Dealing directly with creditors can bring unexpected benefits. In times of financial difficulty, negotiating lower interest rates or more favorable repayment terms can ease the debt burden. Many lenders prefer to work with individuals who have committed to repaying their debts, making negotiation a valuable tool in the debt management arsenal.

7. Seek professional help:

Individuals facing complex or overwhelming debt situations may find it helpful to seek professional advice. Financial advisors or credit counseling services can provide expertise and customized strategies for solving specific problems. Their expertise can empower individuals to make informed decisions and more effectively navigate the path to financial success.

8. Cultivate financial literacy:
Empowerment through financial literacy is integral to long-term financial success. Understanding the principles of budgeting, investing and debt management equips individuals with the knowledge needed to make informed financial decisions. Continuous learning in this area ensures adaptability to the evolving economic environment.
In the pursuit of financial success, effective debt management is a cornerstone. By adopting a holistic approach that includes budgeting, prioritization, and strategic decision-making, individuals can unlock the door to financial freedom. It's not just about eliminating debt; it's about cultivating financial habits that promote resilience, stability and the ability to thrive in an ever-changing economic environment. Through diligence, informed decision-making, and a commitment to financial wellness, individuals can successfully navigate the complexities of debt and embark on a path to lasting financial success.

Chapter 3. Investing Wisely for Long-Term Growth

Investing wisely for long-term growth is a strategic approach that can unlock financial success and provide individuals with a secure financial future. In an ever-changing economic environment, understanding the principles of smart investing is essential to making informed decisions that deliver significant returns over time. This contextual content dives into key aspects of smart investing and highlights the importance of a long-term perspective for sustainable financial growth.

Smart investing is not just about chasing short-term gains or following market trends. It involves a thoughtful and thoughtful approach, aligning investments with long-term goals and financial aspirations. The road to financial success begins with a clear understanding of the basic principles governing intelligent investing.

Setting long-term goals:

One of the basic steps in smart investing is setting clear and realistic long-term financial goals. Whether it's funding a child's education, buying a home or a comfortable retirement, specific goals provide a blueprint for investment decisions. This clarity helps in choosing the right investment instruments that are consistent with the time horizon and risk tolerance associated with each objective.

Diversification as a Risk Mitigation Strategy:

Diversification of investments is a proven strategy for mitigating the risks associated with market volatility. By spreading investments across different asset classes, such as stocks, bonds and real estate, investors can reduce the impact of poor performance of any single investment. Diversification provides a safety net that allows a portfolio to withstand market fluctuations and contribute to long-term growth.

Stay informed and adapt:

Financial markets are dynamic, affected by various factors such as economic conditions, geopolitical events and technological advances. Successful long-term investors are aware of these variables and adjust their investment strategies accordingly. Regular review and adjustment of portfolios ensures that they remain in line with changing market dynamics.

Compounding Income Over Time:
The power of compounding is a key driver of long-term investment success. Reinvesting earnings rather than cashing out allows investors to benefit from a compounding effect where both the earnings from the initial investment and the cumulative returns generate exponential growth. Compounding over a longer period of time can significantly increase your overall return on investment.

Risk tolerance and asset allocation:
Understanding risk tolerance is the foundation for making wise investment decisions. Different individuals have different comfort levels with risk,

and this needs to be taken into account when determining asset allocation. Younger investors with a longer time horizon may choose a more aggressive strategy with a higher allocation to stocks, while those nearing retirement may lean toward a more conservative approach.

Emotional discipline during market fluctuations:
Market volatility is inevitable and emotions often come into play during turbulent times. Sensible long-term investing involves maintaining emotional discipline and not succumbing to impulsive decisions influenced by short-term market trends. Emotional stability allows investors to stay the course during market downturns and avoid panic selling, which can erode long-term growth potential.

Tax Efficient Investing:
Considering the tax implications of investment decisions is a critical aspect of long-term financial planning. Implementing tax-efficient strategies such as taking advantage of tax-advantaged accounts and optimizing the timing of capital gains can

increase overall returns and contribute to sustainable financial growth.

Environmental, Social and Governance (ESG) Investments:
As social values evolve, so does the approach to investing. ESG investing integrates environmental, social and governance factors into investment decisions and aligns portfolios with ethical and sustainable practices. Investing in companies that prioritize responsible business practices not only contributes to a positive social impact, but is also in line with the growing trend of conscious consumerism.

Regular portfolio review and rebalancing:
Regular reviews and rebalancing are necessary to ensure investment portfolios remain aligned with long-term goals. Market movements and changes in personal circumstances may require adjustments to the initial asset allocation. Regularly evaluating investment performance and rebalancing the portfolio helps keep it aligned with the investor's financial goals.

Investing wisely for long-term growth is a dynamic and multifaceted process that goes beyond short-term market speculation. By setting clear goals, diversifying portfolios, staying informed and maintaining emotional discipline, investors can unlock financial success and build a solid foundation for their future. The principles discussed in this contextual content provide a comprehensive guide for individuals who want to navigate the complexities of financial markets and achieve lasting prosperity through smart investing.

3.1 Understanding Investment Vehicles

Investment tools play a key role in unlocking financial success by providing individuals with a variety of opportunities to grow their wealth. Understanding these tools is essential for anyone who wants to navigate the complex world of finance and make informed decisions that align with their financial goals. In this survey, we'll dive into different investment vehicles and explore their features, risks, and potential rewards.

One of the basic investment tools is the stock market. Investing in stocks involves buying shares of publicly traded companies, giving investors a stake in the ownership of those businesses. Stocks have historically provided higher investment returns compared to other asset classes, but come with a certain degree of volatility. Successful investing in the stock market requires a thorough understanding of market trends, company fundamentals and a strategic approach to risk management.

Bonds are another critical investment tool. When an individual buys a bond, they are essentially lending money to the government or corporation in exchange for regular interest payments and the return of the principal at maturity. Bonds are considered less risky than stocks and offer a steady income stream. However, they may not provide the same level of long-term growth potential. Diversifying a portfolio with both stocks and bonds can help manage risk and improve overall stability.

Real estate is a tangible investment vehicle that involves the purchase of real estate with the expectation of generating rental income or appreciating the property's value over time. Real estate investments can provide a source of passive income and serve as a hedge against inflation. However, they also come with the challenges of property management, market volatility and illiquidity.

Mutual funds and exchange-traded funds (ETFs) offer investors a convenient way to access a diversified portfolio without having to pick individual securities. These investment vehicles pool money from multiple investors to invest in a diversified basket of stocks, bonds or other assets. Mutual funds are actively managed, with fund managers making investment decisions, while ETFs typically track an index passively. Both options provide the benefits of diversification and professional management, making them suitable for investors looking for a more hands-on approach.

For those seeking more direct ownership and control of their investments, individual retirement accounts (IRAs) and 401(k) plans are popular vehicles. These tax-advantaged accounts allow individuals to save for retirement while taking advantage of potential tax benefits. Contributions to traditional IRAs and 401(k) plans can be tax-deductible, while Roth IRAs offer tax-free retirement withdrawals. Understanding the nuances of these retirement accounts is key to optimizing tax efficiency and maximizing long-term wealth accumulation.

Cryptocurrencies have emerged as a relatively new and innovative investment tool. Bitcoin, Ethereum and other digital assets have gained popularity for their decentralized nature and potential for high returns. However, the cryptocurrency market is characterized by extreme volatility and regulatory uncertainty, requiring investors to approach it with caution and a thorough understanding of the risks involved.

Precious metals such as gold and silver serve as both investment vehicles and hedges against economic uncertainty. Investors often turn to precious metals as a store of value in times of inflation or geopolitical instability. While they may not generate regular income, these commodities can act as a diversification tool in a well-balanced investment portfolio.

Understanding the trade-off between risk and return is an integral part of successful investing. High-risk investment vehicles such as venture capital and individual stocks have the potential for significant returns, but also come with a higher probability of loss. On the other hand, low-risk options such as government bonds offer more stability but may provide lower returns. The key to unlocking financial success is finding the right balance based on your individual risk tolerance, financial goals and time horizon.

It can be said that orientation in the world of investment instruments is a crucial aspect of achieving financial success. Each type of investment has its own set of characteristics, risks and potential rewards. Diversification, thorough research and a clear understanding of one's financial goals are essential to building a balanced investment portfolio. By comprehensively understanding the intricacies of various investment vehicles, individuals can make informed decisions that align with their financial aspirations and pave the way to long-term prosperity.

3.2 Risk Management and Diversification

In the dynamic environment of personal finance, the path to financial success is marked by uncertainties and challenges. Two key principles that play a key role in navigating this complex terrain are risk management and diversification. This essay examines the symbiotic relationship between risk management, diversification, and achieving financial success.

Understanding Risk Management:
Risk management is the strategic process of identifying, evaluating and mitigating potential risks in order to achieve financial objectives. It includes a comprehensive evaluation of various factors such as market fluctuations, economic downturns and unforeseen events. By recognizing and quantifying these risks, individuals can develop effective strategies to protect their assets and investments.

One of the basic risk management tools is the establishment of an emergency fund. This financial cushion acts as a buffer against unexpected expenses or income shortfalls and provides a safety net to overcome unforeseen challenges without compromising long-term financial goals.

Diversification: Shield against volatility:
Diversification is a principle that advocates spreading investments across different assets to minimize exposure to any single risk. The saying "don't put all your eggs in one basket" sums up the essence of diversification. By dividing assets into different classes such as stocks, bonds, real estate and commodities, individuals can reduce the impact of an underperforming asset on the overall portfolio. Diversification is not only about asset allocation, but also extends to geographic regions, industries and investment strategies. A well-diversified portfolio is less susceptible to market volatility and economic downturns. When one segment of the market experiences a decline, other components can perform better, helping to balance the overall performance of the portfolio.

The interplay between risk management and diversification:

Risk management and diversification are interconnected elements that complement each other in the pursuit of financial success. Effective risk management involves not only identifying risks, but also devising strategies to mitigate them. Diversification serves as one such strategy by spreading investments, naturally reducing the specific risks associated with individual assets.

For example, consider a scenario where an investor has invested heavily in one industry. If the industry faces a downturn, the entire investment portfolio is at risk. However, if an investor practices diversification of fund allocations across different sectors, the impact of a downturn in one sector is mitigated by the positive performance of others.

Strategic asset allocation:

A key aspect of achieving a balanced risk-return profile is strategic asset allocation. This includes determining the optimal mix of asset classes based on individual financial goals, risk tolerance and investment horizon. A well-thought-out asset allocation strategy takes into account the potential returns and risks associated with each asset class, aligning the portfolio with the investor's financial goals.

Rebalancing is an integral part of strategic asset allocation. Regularly reassessing the portfolio and making adjustments based on market conditions ensures that the desired asset allocation is maintained. This proactive approach helps investors stay on course and prevents the portfolio from being overexposed to specific risks.

Real world applications:

To illustrate a practical application of risk management and diversification, consider a hypothetical investor named Sarah. Sarah has a diversified portfolio consisting of stocks, bonds and real estate across various industries and geographies. It also maintains an emergency fund equivalent to six months of living expenses.

When the stock market experiences a downturn, Sarah's portfolio is protected from significant losses through a diversification strategy. At the same time, her emergency fund provides a financial reserve that ensures that she does not have to liquidate investments in adverse times.

In the pursuit of financial success, risk management and diversification are cornerstones that provide stability and resilience. By taking a proactive approach to identifying and mitigating risk, individuals can protect their financial well-being. At the same time, diversification serves as a powerful tool for navigating the unpredictable nature of financial markets and ensures that the path to financial success is characterized by stability and consistent growth. Through careful integration of risk management and diversification, individuals can unlock the full potential of their financial endeavors.

3.3 Setting Investment Goals

Setting investment goals is a crucial step on the road to financial success. In a world where financial stability and growth are highly sought after, strategic investment planning can be critical. This article explores the importance of setting investment goals, the process involved, and the impact it can have on achieving long-term financial success.

Financial success is a universal aspiration, and strategic investment serves as a key driver in realizing this goal. Setting investment goals provides a plan that not only guides individuals but also helps them focus on their financial goals. Whether the goal is to build wealth, fund education, or enjoy a comfortable retirement, well-defined investment goals act as a compass to guide investors through the complexities of the financial landscape.

Importance of setting investment goals

1. Clarity and Focus

Setting investment goals brings clarity to financial aspirations. It forces individuals to articulate their goals, whether short-term gains, long-term growth, or a combination of both. This clarity, in turn, helps in creating a targeted investment strategy in line with specific financial milestones.

2. Risk management

Clear investment objectives enable better risk management. Understanding one's risk tolerance and time horizon becomes easier when there are well-defined goals. This knowledge allows investors to make informed decisions and balance potential returns with an acceptable level of risk.

3. Discipline in Financial Planning

Investing without goals is similar to going on a journey without a destination. Setting investment goals brings discipline to financial planning. It encourages regular reviews and adjustments to ensure that the investment strategy remains in line with evolving life and market conditions.

Investment Goal Setting Process

1. Self-reflection:

The journey begins with self-reflection. Investors must evaluate their financial situation, assess their risk tolerance and determine their investment time horizon. This introspection lays the foundation for setting realistic and achievable investment goals.

2. Define short and long term goals:

Investment goals can be divided into short-term and long-term. Short-term goals might include building an emergency fund or saving for a vacation, while long-term goals might include planning for retirement, buying a home, or financing a child's education. Differentiating between these timelines helps in creating a balanced investment portfolio.

3. Quantify goals:

Assigning specific monetary values to each goal is essential. Whether it's the amount needed for a down payment on a house or a target retirement corpus, quantifying goals provides a clear benchmark to track progress.

4. Consider inflation and market conditions:

A holistic approach includes taking into account inflation and market conditions. Because these variables can affect the purchasing power of money and the return on investment, taking them into account when setting goals ensures that goals are realistic and achievable.

1. Accumulation of wealth:

Setting investment goals accelerates wealth accumulation. With a clear roadmap, investors can systematically contribute to their portfolios and enjoy compounded returns over time. This disciplined approach can greatly enhance the growth of their wealth.

2. Financial security:

Defined investment goals contribute to financial security. Whether it's an emergency safety net or a retirement fund, achieving these goals provides a sense of financial stability and protects individuals from unexpected financial difficulties.

3. Flexibility and adaptability.

While setting investment goals is essential, flexibility is equally important. Life is dynamic and circumstances change. Regularly reassessing goals allows for adjustments based on evolving priorities, market conditions, and personal situations.

4. Empowerment through Education:

The process of setting investment goals is an educational journey. Investors will learn about different asset classes, investment vehicles and market dynamics. This knowledge enables them to make informed decisions, reducing reliance on external advice and mitigating potential risks.

It can be said that setting investment goals is the cornerstone of financial success. It provides direction, promotes discipline and enables individuals to navigate the complex world of investing. Whether the goal is to buy a house, fund a child's education, or have a comfortable retirement, a well-thought-out investment plan increases the likelihood of achieving those goals. As the financial landscape continues to evolve, the importance of setting investment goals remains timeless and offers a surefire path to unlocking long-term financial success.

Chapter 4. Income Generation Strategies

In the pursuit of financial success, individuals often find themselves exploring different income generation strategies to ensure a stable and prosperous future. This journey requires a strategic approach, thoughtful planning and a willingness to adapt to changing economic conditions. This article delves into the realm of income generation strategies and examines their importance in unlocking financial success.

Section 1: Understanding the importance of different income streams:
One of the basic principles of financial success is the creation of various sources of income. Relying on only one source of income can expose an individual to financial vulnerability. Exploring multiple streams such as employment income, investments, side hustles and passive income not

only mitigates risk but also increases overall financial resilience.

Part 2: Traditional employment and career progression:

For many, the traditional 9-to-5 job remains the main source of income. However, unlocking financial success in this area often involves strategic career planning. Constantly developing your skills, networking, and seeking promotion or advancement can greatly increase your earning potential. It is essential to match personal skills and interests with career choices to ensure long-term job satisfaction and financial stability.

Section 3: Investing for Wealth Accumulation:

Investing is the cornerstone of wealth creation and financial success. Whether through stocks, real estate or other investment vehicles, individuals can use the power of compounding to grow their wealth over time. Understanding risk tolerance, conducting thorough research and diversifying investment portfolios are essential components of a successful investment strategy.

Section 4: Business and side hustles:

Businesses and side hustles offer opportunities to supplement income and in some cases become primary sources of income. Starting a small business or freelancing in an area of expertise can provide both financial reward and a sense of independence. However, careful planning, market analysis and a clear understanding of the target group are essential to the success of business activities.

Section 5: Passive Income Streams:

Passive income streams such as dividends, royalties or rental income play a vital role in achieving financial success. These sources of income require initial effort and investment, but can generate returns over a longer period of time with minimal ongoing involvement. Building a diversified portfolio of passive income streams can provide financial stability and create a foundation for long-term wealth.

Section 6: Budgeting and Financial Management:

Effectively managing income is as important as generating it. Budgeting enables individuals to allocate funds wisely, prioritize financial goals, and avoid unnecessary spending. By adopting sound financial management practices, individuals can optimize their income and accelerate their path to financial success.

Section 7: Continuous learning and skills development:

In a dynamic and ever-evolving labor market, continuous learning and skill development is essential. Staying relevant in your field or acquiring new skills can open the door to better job opportunities, higher paying positions or entrepreneurial pursuits. Investing in education and personal development is an essential part of a comprehensive income generation strategy.

Unlocking financial success is a multi-faceted journey that requires a combination of strategic planning, adaptability and proactive decision-making. Diversifying income streams, investing wisely, exploring business opportunities and practicing effective financial management are key elements of this effort. By understanding the importance of various income generation strategies and incorporating them into a personalized financial plan, individuals can navigate the path to financial success with confidence and resilience.

4.1 Career Advancement and Skill Development

In the dynamic environment of the modern workforce, the pursuit of financial success is intricately linked to career progression and skill development. As the industry evolves and technology changes the way we work, individuals must proactively invest in improving their skills to stay relevant and climb the career ladder. This symbiotic relationship between professional growth and financial prosperity forms the basis of a thriving and fulfilling career.

The changing landscape of work:
The traditional career path has undergone a significant transformation in recent years. Gone are the days of linear career paths where individuals

entered a company, steadily climbed the ranks, and retired after decades of service. Today, the labor market is characterized by rapid changes that are driven by technological progress, globalization and the gig economy.

In order to successfully navigate this dynamic environment, individuals must embrace continuous learning and skill development. Career advancement is no longer dependent on tenure alone; rather, it is influenced by one's ability to adapt to change, acquire new skills, and demonstrate commitment to personal and professional growth.

Investing in Yourself: The Power of Skill Development:

At the heart of career progression is the concept of skill development. Acquiring and improving relevant skills not only makes individuals more competitive in the labor market, but also equips them to make meaningful contributions to their organizations. This proactive approach to upskilling serves as a catalyst for career progression and opens doors to new opportunities.

In the digital age, technological literacy is the cornerstone of professional success. Whether it's mastering data analytics tools, programming languages, or keeping up with the latest advances in artificial intelligence, individuals who invest in developing technical skills become valuable assets in a technology-based workforce.

In addition to technical knowledge, soft skills such as communication, adaptability and problem solving play a key role in career progression. As professionals take on more complex roles and leadership positions, the ability to effectively collaborate, manage challenges and lead teams becomes increasingly important.

Career Progression: Climbing the Ladder with Purpose:

Career progression is not just about climbing the hierarchical ladder; it is about intentional and strategic growth. Individuals must cultivate a proactive mindset, seek opportunities for professional development and networking. Participating in mentorship programs, attending industry conferences, and pursuing advanced degrees are all ways professionals can accelerate their careers.

In addition, demonstrating leadership qualities can significantly influence career progression. Taking on leadership roles, leading projects and demonstrating the ability to drive positive change in an organization are key indicators of leadership potential. Employers are often looking for individuals who not only excel in their roles, but also inspire and motivate others.

Financial implications of career progression:

As professionals move up the career ladder through skill development and strategic advancement, the financial implications become more pronounced. Senior-level roles typically come with more responsibility and, as a result, larger compensation packages. Salary increases, bonuses, and other benefits are common rewards for those who show consistent growth and make significant contributions to their organizations.

In addition, career advancement often opens the door to new job opportunities with organizations willing to offer competitive compensation for top talent. Negotiating salary and benefits becomes a key skill at this stage, and individuals who can effectively communicate their value to potential employers are well positioned to secure lucrative working conditions.

Finding balance: career progression, skills development and work-life balance:

While the pursuit of career advancement and financial success is essential, it is equally important to find a balance that promotes overall well-being. The concept of work-life harmony came to the fore as individuals realized the importance of maintaining a healthy balance between professional and personal interests.

Investing in skills development doesn't have to be an onerous task; it can be a fulfilling journey of self-discovery and growth. Continuous learning can be integrated into the daily routine through online courses, workshops and mentoring relationships. Balancing career ambitions with personal priorities ensures that individuals not only move up the career ladder, but also lead fulfilling lives outside the workplace.

A Holistic Approach to Success:

The interplay between career progression, skill development and financial success forms the basis of a successful and fulfilling career path. The modern workforce requires adaptability, a commitment to lifelong learning and a strategic approach to climbing the career ladder. By investing in themselves, cultivating a growth mindset, and taking advantage of opportunities for advancement, individuals can unlock the door to financial prosperity and build a career that aligns with their aspirations. In this dynamic age, success is not a goal, but a constant path of evolution and self-improvement.

4.2 Passive Income Streams

In the ever-evolving landscape of personal finance, the pursuit of financial success takes many forms. One key aspect that is gaining more and more attention is the concept of passive income streams. These income streams have become a cornerstone for individuals seeking financial independence and offer a path that differs from the traditional nine-to-five job model. In this survey, we'll delve into the world of passive income, explore its importance in unlocking financial success, and the various avenues through which it can be achieved.

Understanding passive income:
Passive income is income earned with minimal effort or direct involvement. Unlike active income derived from a traditional job that requires continuous work to generate earnings, passive income is generated through investments, business ventures, or assets that operate autonomously. The allure of passive income lies in its potential to create a steady and reliable cash flow that allows individuals to break free from the constraints of time and conventional employment structures.

Diversification of income streams:
Financial success often depends on the ability to diversify sources of income. Passive income provides a means to achieve this diversification, reducing reliance on a single income stream and increasing overall financial resilience. Diversification not only protects against economic

uncertainty, but also opens up opportunities for growth and wealth accumulation.

Investment portfolios, real estate, royalties and business ownership are among the countless sources of passive income. Each path presents unique opportunities and challenges, allowing individuals to tailor a passive income strategy based on their preferences, risk tolerance and financial goals.

Real estate: Pillar of passive income:

Real estate stands out as a typical avenue for passive income. Investing in real estate, whether through rental properties or real estate crowdfunding platforms, offers the potential for regular rental income and property appreciation. Real estate's ability to generate passive income makes it a popular choice for those looking for long-term financial success.

However, the real estate market requires careful consideration and research. Understanding market trends, evaluating potential returns and effective property management are essential components of a successful real estate investment strategy.

Investment portfolios and dividends:

Investing in stocks, bonds and other financial instruments can also contribute to passive income. In particular, dividend-paying stocks offer a consistent stream of income as companies share profits with shareholders. Building a well-balanced investment portfolio in line with your risk tolerance and financial goals can provide a reliable source of passive income.

The inherent volatility of the stock market requires a strategic and informed approach. Diversification of investments, monitoring of market trends and adoption of a long-term perspective are necessary to navigate the complexity of financial markets.

Entrepreneurship and Business Ownership:

While entrepreneurship often requires active involvement in the early stages, building a successful business can eventually lead to passive income. Automated business processes, franchise ownership, and online business are examples of business-related passive income streams. In particular, the scalability of online business allows entrepreneurs to reach a global audience and generate income even while they sleep.

Starting and sustaining a business requires dedication, resilience and strategic planning. Identifying market needs, developing effective systems, and promoting a brand that resonates with consumers are critical elements in creating a passive income stream through your business.

Intellectual Property and License Fees:
Creativity and innovation can be a lucrative source of passive income through the creation of intellectual property. For example, authors, musicians, and artists may receive royalties for books, music, or artwork long after it was first created. The digital age has expanded these opportunities with platforms that facilitate the monetization of creative works around the world.

Protection of intellectual property rights and efficient use of distribution channels are essential factors for those who want to turn their creative efforts into sustainable sources of passive income.

The importance of continuous learning:

Achieving financial success through passive income requires a commitment to constant learning and adaptation. Markets evolve, the economic landscape changes, and technological advances create new opportunities. Being informed about investment strategies, market trends and new technologies is essential to optimizing your passive income streams.

In the pursuit of financial success, integrating passive income streams is a powerful strategy. Diversifying income sources through real estate, investments, business and intellectual property can provide stability, resilience and the potential for exponential growth. However, it is essential to approach passive income with a clear understanding of the risks involved, a commitment to continuous education and a strategic mindset. By unlocking the potential of passive income, individuals can chart a path to financial success that transcends the boundaries of traditional employment and takes advantage of the opportunities of a dynamic and evolving financial environment.

4.3 Entrepreneurial Ventures

Entrepreneurial ventures serve as dynamic pathways to unlocking financial success by leveraging innovation, seizing opportunities, and navigating challenges. These businesses embody the spirit of risk-taking and inventive problem-solving, creating fertile ground for economic growth and individual prosperity.

Successful entrepreneurs often demonstrate a keen ability to identify market gaps, envision new solutions, and turn their ideas into viable businesses. Through strategic planning and adaptability, they navigate the uncertainties of business and turn obstacles into stepping stones to financial success.

Innovation is the cornerstone of business activities. Entrepreneurs are constantly looking for disruptive ideas, disruptive technologies or unique business models that can differentiate them from the competition. This commitment to innovation not only moves an entrepreneur's business forward, but also contributes to the overall progress of industries and economies.

In addition, the ability to take advantage of opportunities plays a key role in the financial success of entrepreneurial activities. Entrepreneurs are very good at recognizing market trends, consumer needs and emerging technologies, which allows them to position their businesses advantageously. Whether it's capitalizing on a niche market or adapting quickly to changing circumstances, these businesses thrive by being proactive and responsive.

Building a successful business venture also requires effective financial management. Entrepreneurs must allocate resources judiciously, balance budgets and seek sustainable sources of income. Access to capital, whether through investments, loans or strategic partnerships, is often a critical factor in scaling a business and ensuring long-term financial viability.

Moreover, the impact of entrepreneurial activities goes beyond individual success and contributes significantly to job creation, economic development and community empowerment. Successful entrepreneurs often become catalysts for positive change, inspiring others to realize their aspirations and fostering a culture of innovation and resilience. Entrepreneurial activities serve as dynamic engines for unlocking financial success. Through innovation, taking advantage of opportunities and effective financial management, entrepreneurs navigate the complexity of the business environment and achieve not only personal prosperity, but also contribute to the overall economic well-being of society.

Chapter 5. Financial Literacy and Education

Financial literacy and education play a key role in achieving financial success for individuals and communities. At a time when the economic landscape is dynamic and financial decisions are increasingly complex, the ability to understand and manage your finances is more important than ever. This contextual survey delves into the importance of financial literacy, its impact on personal and societal prosperity, and the various ways in which financial literacy education can promote economic empowerment.

Financial literacy includes the knowledge and skills needed to make informed and effective financial decisions. It goes beyond basic budgeting and expands to understanding complex financial instruments, investing, debt management and retirement planning. Individuals who are equipped with financial literacy are better able to navigate the complex web of personal finance, ensure proper decision-making and prudent allocation of resources.

The connection between financial literacy and success is profound. One of the basic aspects is the ability to budget effectively. Financially literate individuals understand the importance of creating and following a budget that allows them to manage expenses, save for future goals, and avoid unnecessary debt. This basic skill paves the way for more advanced financial strategies and investments that allow individuals to accumulate wealth over time.

Additionally, financial literacy enables individuals to make informed investment decisions. Understanding the intricacies of stocks, bonds and other financial instruments allows them to create diversified portfolios that are consistent with their risk tolerance and financial goals. This knowledge makes them less likely to fall victim to fraudulent schemes and dubious investment practices and protects their hard-earned money.

Financial literacy education is especially important when it comes to debt management. Many individuals face problems related to loans, credit cards and mortgages. Financial literacy equips individuals with the tools to understand the implications of taking on debt and enables them to make informed decisions about borrowing and repayment. This in turn prevents the accumulation of unsustainable debt that can hinder financial progress.

Beyond individual impact, a financially literate population contributes to the overall economic health of communities and nations. When people make sound financial decisions, they are less likely to rely on social safety nets, reducing the burden on public resources. Moreover, financially savvy individuals are more likely to contribute to economic growth through responsible spending, investment and entrepreneurship.

Financial education also plays a key role in addressing economic disparities. Access to quality financial education can break the cycle of poverty by giving individuals the tools to escape financial vulnerability. By understanding how to save, invest and plan for the future, marginalized communities can improve their economic prospects and contribute to the overall development of society.

Schools, colleges and community organizations play an integral role in spreading financial education. Incorporating financial literacy into the curriculum equips students with essential life skills and prepares them for the complex financial decisions they will face as adults. Additionally, community programs and workshops ensure that individuals across age groups and backgrounds have access to financial education.

However, problems persist in ensuring widespread financial literacy. There is a need for comprehensive and accessible learning resources that cater to different learning styles and demographics. Governments, financial institutions and non-profit organizations must work together to develop and implement effective financial education initiatives. These efforts should prioritize inclusivity and ensure that marginalized groups have equal access to educational resources.

Financial literacy and education are indispensable tools for achieving financial success. Empowering individuals with the knowledge and skills to make informed financial decisions not only increases their personal prosperity, but also contributes to the economic well-being of society as a whole. By prioritizing financial education at the individual, institutional and societal levels, we can pave the way for a future where financial success is within everyone's reach.

5.1 Importance of Financial Education

Financial education plays a key role in enabling individuals to navigate the complex landscape of personal finance and ultimately unlock financial success. In a world where economic uncertainties are the norm, understanding the principles of financial management becomes essential for individuals seeking stability and prosperity.

One of the key aspects of financial education is budgeting. Many people find themselves in a precarious financial situation due to a lack of understanding of budgeting. Financial education equips individuals with the knowledge and skills to create and stick to a budget, ensuring that income is appropriately allocated to cover necessary expenses, save for the future, and even invest wisely. This basic skill forms the cornerstone of financial success by promoting disciplined and strategic money management.

In addition, financial education instills in individuals a sense of responsibility and accountability for their financial decisions. It encourages them to critically evaluate their spending and make informed decisions about saving and investing. Understanding the consequences of financial decisions allows individuals to make decisions that align with their long-term goals and steer them away from impulsive or harmful financial behavior.

Investing is another critical part of financial success, yet many individuals avoid it due to a lack of understanding. Financial education demystifies the world of investing, explaining concepts such as risk, diversification and compound interest. Armed with this knowledge, individuals can make informed investment decisions that have the potential to grow their wealth over time, a critical factor in achieving financial success.

In addition to personal financial management, financial education plays a vital role in preparing individuals for unforeseen circumstances. Understanding insurance, emergency funds, and risk mitigation strategies ensures that individuals are not financially devastated by unexpected events such as emergencies or job loss. This proactive approach to risk management is a key element in securing your own financial future.

In addition, financial education contributes to the development of a saving mindset. It emphasizes the importance of setting aside a portion of income for future needs and goals. Whether you're saving for education, housing, or retirement, having a savings mindset is essential to achieving financial milestones. Financial education equips individuals with the tools to set realistic savings goals, create a systematic savings plan, and maintain long-term financial goals.

In the modern age, when technology is moving fast, financial education also includes digital literacy. Understanding online banking, digital payments and cyber security is critical to protecting financial assets and navigating the evolving financial technology landscape. Without sufficient digital literacy, individuals can become victims of fraud or miss out on the opportunities offered by digital financial tools.

In addition, financial education contributes to the overall economic well-being of society. A population that is well-versed in financial principles is more likely to make sound economic decisions, which will contribute to a stable and prosperous economy. It reduces the burden on social support systems by promoting the financial independence and resilience of individuals.

The importance of financial education in unlocking financial success cannot be overstated. From budgeting and investing to risk management and digital literacy, well-rounded financial education empowers individuals to make informed and strategic decisions about their finances. By fostering a sense of responsibility, instilling a frugal mindset and promoting digital literacy, financial education lays the foundation for a secure and prosperous financial future. It is an investment in oneself that pays off over a lifetime and ensures not only individual success, but also contributes to the overall economic health of society.

5.2 Keeping Up with Market Trends

Keeping up with market trends is critical to achieving financial success in today's dynamic business environment. In an ever-evolving market, being constantly attuned to changes and patterns can be the key difference between financial prosperity and stagnation.

Market trends encompass a wide range of factors, from consumer preferences and technological advances to global economic conditions. A good understanding of these trends is essential for both businesses and investors. It not only enables proactive decision-making, but also provides a competitive advantage in exploiting opportunities and mitigating risks.

One of the main reasons to keep up with market trends is to identify emerging opportunities. Industries are constantly evolving, driven by innovation and changing consumer needs. By keeping up with market trends, businesses can tap into new areas of growth. For example, the rise of e-commerce and the shift to sustainable products are trends that have created lucrative opportunities for early adopters.

Additionally, being informed about market trends helps in risk management. Economic downturns, geopolitical events or technological disruptions can affect the industry in unexpected ways. Being aware of these trends allows businesses to implement preventative measures, diversify portfolios and strengthen financial structures. This proactive approach increases resilience and protects against potential setbacks.

Keeping up with market trends is crucial when it comes to investing. Financial markets are affected by a number of factors such as interest rates, inflation and geopolitical events. Investors who are well versed in market trends can make informed asset allocation decisions and optimize their portfolios for current conditions. This knowledge also helps in identifying undervalued assets or sectors poised for growth.

In addition, market trends provide valuable insights into consumer behavior. Understanding what drives purchasing decisions enables businesses to adapt their products and services to meet evolving demands. This customer-centric approach not only fosters brand loyalty, but also ensures consistent revenue growth. For example, the trend towards digitization has forced businesses to improve their online presence and simplify the customer experience.

In the context of technology, keeping up with market trends is essential for businesses that want to stay competitive. Innovations such as artificial intelligence, blockchain and the Internet of Things are reshaping industries. Companies that adopt these technologies gain a strategic advantage, improve operational efficiency and create innovative solutions. Failure to adapt to technological trends can result in obsolescence and missed opportunities.

Global economic trends also play a key role in financial success. The interconnectedness of economies means that events in one part of the world can have global effects. For example, changes in trade policy, currency fluctuations or geopolitical tensions can affect markets and industries. Businesses that monitor these macroeconomic trends can adjust their strategies accordingly and mitigate potential disruptions.

Keeping up with market trends is essential to achieving financial success. Whether in business or investment, the ability to anticipate changes in consumer behavior, technology and the broader economic environment is a strategic advantage. Enables proactive decision-making, risk mitigation and identification of new opportunities. In today's fast-paced and connected world, the mantra is clear: those who keep up with market trends are better positioned for financial prosperity.

5.3 Continual Learning for Financial Success

In the ever-evolving landscape of personal finance, the concept of continuous learning has emerged as a key driver of financial success. In a world where economic dynamics, investment strategies, and financial instruments are constantly changing, individuals committed to continuous education position themselves to effectively navigate these complexities. This article explores the profound impact of continuous learning on financial success, exploring how it enables individuals to make informed decisions, adapt to economic shifts, and ultimately build lasting prosperity.

The dynamic nature of finance:
Financial markets are dynamic and subject to constant change. New technologies, geopolitical events and economic shifts can rapidly change the financial landscape, presenting both opportunities and challenges. Continuous education becomes a necessity in this context and serves as a tool to stay informed about market trends, emerging investment opportunities and potential risks.

Informed decision making:
Continuous learning equips individuals with the knowledge needed to make informed financial decisions. Whether it's understanding the intricacies of various investment instruments, understanding the implications of economic policy, or staying up-to-date on tax regulations, continuing education provides the knowledge you need to

make the right decisions. Informed choices help preserve and grow wealth over time.

Adaptability in the face of change:
The financial world is no stranger to uncertainty. Economic downturns, market volatility and unforeseen events can disrupt even the most carefully laid financial plans. Continuous learning promotes adaptability and allows individuals to adapt their strategies in response to changing circumstances. This adaptability is a critical element in mitigating risks and seizing opportunities as they arise.

Developing Skills for Financial Mastery:
Financial success often depends on the mastery of various skills. From budgeting and investment analysis to risk management and negotiation, navigating the complexities of personal finance requires a broad skill set. Continuous learning enables individuals to hone these skills and foster a level of financial mastery that increases their ability to achieve and sustain success.

Investment strategy and portfolio management:

The investment field is multifaceted, with different asset classes, risk profiles and investment strategies. Continuous learning enables individuals to refine their understanding of these components and facilitates the creation and management of balanced and diversified portfolios. A strategic approach to investing, guided by up-to-date knowledge, is essential to achieving long-term financial goals.

Use of technological progress:

The integration of technology into finance is changing the way individuals manage their money. Fintech innovations, robo-advisors and blockchain technologies are reshaping traditional financial systems. Continuous learning helps individuals harness the power of these improvements, enabling them to optimize financial processes, reduce costs and access new investment opportunities.

Financial literacy and empowerment:

Financial literacy is the cornerstone of continuous learning for financial success. Understanding financial concepts, terms and tools empowers individuals to take control of their financial destinies. A literate individual is better equipped to make strategic decisions, plan for the future, and navigate the complex web of available financial options.

Networking and collaborative learning:
The financial environment is not just about individual effort on collaboration and networking. Continuous learning fosters connections within the financial community, creating opportunities for knowledge exchange, mentorship and collaboration. Through these networks, individuals can gain valuable insights, share experiences, and stay abreast of industry trends.

Overcoming behavioral biases:
Behavioral biases can hinder sound financial decision-making. Continuous learning helps individuals recognize and overcome these biases and promotes a disciplined and rational approach

to money management. By understanding the psychological pitfalls, individuals can make financial decisions that align with their long-term goals rather than succumbing to emotional impulses.

Mindfulness in Wealth Building:
Continuous learning goes beyond acquiring technical knowledge; cultivates a wealth-building mindset. This mindset includes taking a proactive approach to financial planning, setting ambitious but realistic goals, and maintaining discipline in the pursuit of financial success. It encourages individuals to view failures as learning opportunities and to persevere in the face of challenges.

A commitment to continuous learning emerges as a fundamental pillar on the road to financial success. It is the tool that propels individuals forward in a dynamic financial environment, providing the tools needed to make informed decisions, adapt to change, and build a foundation for lasting prosperity. When individuals embrace an ethos of lifelong learning, they unlock the potential to not only navigate the complexities of finance, but thrive in an ever-evolving economic environment.

Chapter 6. Building and Protecting Wealth

Building and protecting wealth is a multifaceted journey that goes beyond the accumulation of financial assets. It involves strategic planning, disciplined decision-making and a holistic approach to one's financial well-being. To unlock true financial success, individuals must navigate the complexities of wealth creation and protect their assets from potential risks.

The basis of financial success:
Creating a solid foundation is at the heart of building wealth. This starts with setting clear financial goals and creating a realistic plan to achieve them. Whether it's saving for a home, financing education, or preparing for retirement, a well-defined plan serves as a guide throughout the wealth-building process.

Investments play a key role in wealth creation. Diversification across different asset classes such as stocks, bonds and real estate mitigates risks and increases potential returns. However, it is essential to match investments with individual risk tolerance and time horizon. Regular review and adjustment of the investment portfolio ensures that it remains aligned with evolving financial goals.

The importance of budgeting and savings:
Building wealth takes discipline, and that discipline starts with budgeting. Creating and following a budget allows individuals to effectively allocate resources and ensure that a portion of income goes toward savings and investments. This not only facilitates the accumulation of wealth but also acts as a safety net during unforeseen circumstances.

Savings, especially in emergency funds, provide financial resilience. Having a pool of funds readily available can help weather unexpected expenses without compromising long-term financial goals. It also alleviates the need to rely on debt during challenging times, protecting wealth and minimizing financial stress.

Strategic debt management:

While debt is often seen as an obstacle to building wealth, strategic debt management can be a powerful tool. Leveraging debt for investments that have the potential to generate returns in excess of the cost of borrowing can accelerate wealth accumulation. However, it is essential to distinguish between "good" and "bad" debt, the former contributing to wealth creation and the latter hindering financial progress.

Clearing high-interest debt should be a priority, as it minimizes leakage of funds and frees up resources for more productive use. Developing a debt repayment strategy is consistent with the goal of gradually building wealth.

Risk reduction and asset protection:

Wealth protection requires a thorough awareness of potential risks. Insurance, which offers a safety net against unforeseen events, plays a vital role in this regard. Adequate health, life, property and income coverage is a guarantee against financial setbacks that could otherwise erode wealth.

Estate planning is another critical aspect of wealth protection. Establishing wills, trusts and power of attorney documents ensures a smooth transfer of assets and minimizes tax implications. This future-oriented approach not only secures one's inheritance, but also protects beneficiaries from unnecessary financial burdens.

Constant learning and adaptation:
The financial environment is dynamic and successful wealth builders must remain adaptable. Continuous learning about financial markets, investment strategies and evolving economic conditions enables individuals to make informed decisions. Keeping up with changes in tax laws and financial regulations enables proactive adjustments to wealth management strategies.

Networking with financial professionals and seeking advice when needed is a prudent approach. Professionals such as financial advisors, accountants and estate planners can provide valuable insights tailored to individual circumstances and enhance your overall wealth building strategy.

Emotional intelligence and behavioral finance:

Emotions often play a significant role in financial decision-making. Understanding your own risk tolerance, managing your emotions during market swings, and avoiding impulsive decisions all contribute to long-term financial success. Behavioral finance principles emphasize the importance of emotional intelligence in building wealth and encourage individuals to align their financial decisions with rational, well-thought-out plans.

Building generational wealth:

True financial success goes beyond individual accomplishments to create generational wealth. Passing on financial knowledge, values and a solid financial foundation to future generations ensures a lasting legacy. Establishing trusts, educational funds and fostering a culture of responsible financial management in the family increases the potential for lasting prosperity.

Building and protecting wealth is not a one-size-fits-all endeavor. It requires a personal approach that combines strategic planning, disciplined execution and a commitment to continuous learning. By setting clear goals, disciplined saving and investing, strategic debt management, risk mitigation, and adapting to changing circumstances, individuals can unlock the door to lasting financial success. By doing so, they not only secure their own financial future, but also pave the way for the prosperity of future geStrategies

6.1 Wealth Accumulation Strategies

Accumulating wealth is a multifaceted journey that involves deliberate planning, disciplined habits, and strategic decision-making. Unlocking financial success through effective wealth accumulation strategies requires a comprehensive understanding of the financial landscape and commitment to long-term goals.

One of the key aspects of wealth accumulation is budgeting. Creating a detailed budget serves as a foundation for financial success. It allows individuals to track income, allocate funds for necessary expenses, and identify opportunities for savings and investment. By having a clear idea of where the money is going, individuals can make informed decisions that will contribute to their wealth building journey.

Savings play a key role in wealth accumulation. Establishing an emergency fund provides a financial safety net that protects individuals from unexpected expenses and allows them to avoid dipping into investments or debt during challenging times. Consistent savings contributions promote financial resilience and create a solid financial foundation for future endeavors.

Smart investing is another key strategy for wealth accumulation. Diversifying investment portfolios across different asset classes helps mitigate risks and increase potential returns. Whether it's stocks, bonds, real estate or other investment vehicles, a balanced and diversified approach can yield long-term gains. Regular review and adjustment of investment strategies based on market conditions and personal financial goals is essential for continued success.

Strategic debt management is also an integral part of wealth accumulation. While some types of debt, such as home mortgages, can be considered investments, high-interest consumer debt can hinder financial progress. Prioritizing paying off high-interest debt frees up resources that can be redirected to savings and investments, speeding up the wealth-building process.

Education and continuous learning are powerful tools on the road to financial success. Staying informed about market trends, investment opportunities and personal finance strategies allows individuals to make informed decisions. Attend workshops, read financial literature, and seek advice from renowned financial experts to increase your financial literacy and make more confident decisions.

Entrepreneurship can be a game changer in wealth accumulation. Starting and growing a business can provide additional income streams and create opportunities for significant wealth creation. However, running a business involves risk, and thorough research and planning are essential to mitigate potential problems.

Investing in real estate is a proven wealth accumulation strategy. Property values tend to appreciate over time and rental income can provide a steady cash flow. Understanding the real estate market, location analysis and prudent financial management are key to success in this area.

Retirement planning is a long-term wealth accumulation strategy that cannot be overlooked. Contributing consistently to retirement accounts such as 401(k)s or IRAs ensures financial security in later years. Taking advantage of employer-sponsored retirement plans and maximizing contributions can significantly affect the size of one's retirement nest egg.

Estate planning is the final piece of the wealth accumulation puzzle. Creating a comprehensive estate plan ensures that wealth is effectively passed down to future generations, minimizing tax implications and legal complexities. This strategic approach to wealth transfer preserves financial legacy and provides for loved ones.

Wealth accumulation strategies are essential to achieving financial success. By adopting budgeting, savings, strategic investing, debt management, continuous learning, entrepreneurship, real estate investing, retirement planning, and estate planning, individuals can navigate the path to financial prosperity. The key is to take a holistic and disciplined approach and make informed decisions that align with long-term financial goals.

6.2 Tax Planning and Optimization

Tax planning and optimization play a key role in the path to financial success. By strategically managing their tax affairs, individuals and businesses can unlock countless opportunities to improve their financial well-being. This process involves a comprehensive understanding of tax laws, financial goals, and prudent decision-making to minimize tax liability legally and ethically.

Tax planning is essentially the art of arranging your financial affairs in such a way as to maximize the benefits while minimizing the tax burden. It goes beyond simply complying with tax regulations; it aims to capitalize on available incentives, credits and deductions. The main goal is to preserve wealth and create a more robust financial foundation.

For individuals, tax planning often begins with an assessment of various sources of income.

Understanding the tax implications of earned income, investments and other financial transactions is essential. This awareness enables individuals to make informed decisions about when to realize profits, manage losses, and strategically time significant financial events. For example, the right timing of the sale of assets or investments can lead to substantial tax savings.

Investment choices are also an integral part of effective tax planning. The use of tax-advantaged accounts, such as Individual Retirement Accounts (IRAs) or 401(k)s, allows individuals to grow their wealth in a tax-efficient manner. Additionally, diversifying investments across different asset classes can help balance tax impacts and optimize overall returns.

Entrepreneurs and business owners face a unique set of challenges and opportunities in tax planning. Choosing the right business structure, such as a sole proprietorship, partnership, corporation, or limited liability company (LLC), can significantly affect tax obligations. Each structure has its own tax implications, which are influenced by factors such as income distribution, liability protection, and ease of administration.

Strategic business expenses and deductions also contribute to effective tax planning for businesses. Identifying eligible deductions, such as those related to research and development, equipment purchases or employee benefits, can lead to substantial tax savings. Additionally, understanding the tax breaks available for certain industries or activities can further optimize a business's financial position.

Real estate transactions present another level of tax planning complexity. Whether buying, selling or renting real estate, the tax implications can be significant. Taking advantage of tax advantages such as depreciation, 1031 exchanges, or capital gains strategies can be helpful in maximizing after-tax gains in real estate transactions.

One of the key aspects of tax optimization is keeping up with changes in tax laws. Tax regulations are dynamic and subject to revisions, making it essential for individuals and businesses to adapt their strategies accordingly. Working with tax professionals or financial advisors who have up-to-date knowledge can be helpful in navigating the complex tax planning landscape.

In addition, estate planning is an integral part of long-term tax optimization. Developing a thoughtful estate plan not only ensures a smooth transfer of assets to heirs, but also minimizes potential estate taxes. Tools such as trusts, gift strategies and life insurance can be used to structure assets in a tax-efficient manner.

In the pursuit of financial success, tax planning is not a one-time event, but an ongoing process. Regular reviews of financial goals, income streams and tax strategies are essential to adapt to changing circumstances. Reassessing and adjusting your tax plan as life evolves ensures it stays in line with individual or business goals.

Tax planning and optimization serve as powerful tools on the way to financial success. By carefully examining and managing the financial environment, individuals and businesses can open up opportunities for wealth preservation and growth. The dynamic nature of tax laws requires a proactive and strategic approach, guided by a deep understanding of personal or business financial goals. As taxpayers navigate the complex web of regulations, they pave the way for a more secure and prosperous financial future.

6.3 Estate Planning for Future Generations

Estate planning is a crucial aspect of financial management that goes far beyond simply distributing assets upon death. It is a strategic and thoughtful process aimed at securing the financial future of the family across generations. In this survey, we delve into the importance of estate planning as the key to unlocking financial success for generations to come.

1. Definition and Meaning of Estate Planning:
Estate planning involves carefully arranging assets and property over their lifetime to ensure a smooth transition to the next generation. The primary goal is to minimize any taxes, facilitate the efficient distribution of assets and ensure the financial well-being of the heirs. Importantly, estate planning

is not exclusive to the rich; it is a prudent measure for individuals at all income levels.

2. The Role of Inheritance in Financial Success:
Legacy is a powerful concept in the context of estate planning. In addition to material wealth, it includes the values, wisdom and principles that guide the family. A well-crafted estate plan not only passes on financial assets, but also passes on a legacy that can support financial success for generations to come.

3. Strategic Wealth Transfer:
One of the main components of estate planning is the transfer of wealth. This includes deciding how the property will be divided among the heirs. Using tools such as wills, trusts and beneficiary designations, individuals can strategically transfer wealth while taking into account factors such as taxation, family dynamics and the financial needs of beneficiaries.

4. Tax Efficiency Strategy:

Estate tax can pose a significant threat to the financial legacy you intend to leave. Estate planning includes strategies to minimize tax liability, such as setting up trusts, charitable giving, and taking advantage of exemptions. By understanding and implementing these strategies, individuals can protect a more substantial portion of their wealth for future generations.

5. Property protection:
In addition to asset transfer and tax considerations, estate planning includes asset protection. This includes protection against potential legal issues, creditors and unforeseen financial crises. Establishing structures such as family limited partnerships or limited liability companies can add a layer of protection to family assets.

6. Education and Empowerment:
True financial success goes beyond monetary wealth; includes knowledge and empowerment. Estate planning offers an opportunity to educate future generations about financial responsibility, investment strategies and the importance of

preserving a family legacy. Establishing educational trusts or mentoring programs as part of an estate plan can contribute to the long-term success of heirs.

7. Charitable donations and social impact:
Many individuals view estate planning not only as a means to benefit their family, but also as a way to make a positive impact on society. By incorporating charitable giving into their plans, individuals can create a lasting legacy that extends beyond their immediate family and foster a sense of social responsibility in future generations.

8. Adaptability to changing circumstances:
A well-crafted estate plan is not static; it evolves with changing circumstances. Life events such as births, marriages or changes in financial circumstances may require adjustments to the plan. Regular reviews and updates ensure that the estate plan remains aligned with the family's current goals and the prevailing legal and economic environment.

9. Professional estate planning advice:

Due to the complexity involved, seeking professional advice is paramount in estate planning. Lawyers, financial advisors and tax specialists play a key role in creating a comprehensive plan that aligns with individual goals and ensures effective implementation.

Blueprint for Financial Success:
Estate planning serves as a blueprint for financial success across generations. It is not only about dividing assets, but also about preserving family values, protecting against financial threats and empowering heirs. By navigating the complexities of wealth transfer, tax efficiency and adaptability to change, individuals can unlock legacies that extend far beyond monetary wealth, ensuring a lasting impact on future generations.

Conclusion

Unlocking financial success is a multifaceted journey that goes beyond simply accumulating wealth. It involves a holistic approach involving financial literacy, strategic planning, disciplined savings, prudent investing and opportunity thinking. Understanding the intricacies of personal finance is essential because it allows individuals to make informed decisions that align with their long-term goals.

Financial literacy serves as a foundation for success. It includes gaining knowledge about budgeting, saving, investing and understanding the various financial instruments available. Educating yourself about economic trends, market forces, and the impact of global events on finances empowers individuals to navigate a complex financial environment with confidence.

Strategic planning is a key element in the pursuit of financial success. Setting clear and realistic financial goals provides a blueprint for decision-making. Whether your focus is on home ownership, retirement or business, a well-defined plan ensures that resources are allocated efficiently and progress can be measured. Regularly reassessing and adjusting these plans in response to life changes or shifting priorities is critical to long-term success.

Disciplined saving is the cornerstone of wealth accumulation. Cultivating the habit of saving, even if it's a modest percentage of your income, creates a financial cushion for unforeseen circumstances and lays the foundation for investments. Automating savings through payroll deductions or automated transfers ensures consistency and minimizes the temptation to overspend.

Smart investing is a key driver of financial success. Diversifying investments across different asset classes such as stocks, bonds and real estate helps manage risk and maximize returns. Understanding risk tolerance and time horizon is essential in selecting appropriate investment instruments. Regular checking and balancing of the investment portfolio ensures compliance with financial goals and market conditions.

Adopting a growth mindset is essential to unlocking financial success. Accepting challenges, learning from failures, and viewing setbacks as opportunities for growth fosters resilience to economic uncertainties. Constantly learning about personal finance and following industry trends allows individuals to take advantage of emerging opportunities.

Networking and building relationships within the financial community can provide valuable insights and open doors to potential collaborations or investment opportunities. Learning from successful individuals, seeking mentorship and engaging in discussions about financial strategies can offer new perspectives and improve financial acumen.

Understanding the psychological aspects of money is equally important. Emotional intelligence plays a role in financial decision-making, as impulsive or fear-driven choices can undermine long-term success. Developing emotional resilience and maintaining a balanced approach to both success and failure contributes to a healthier relationship with money.

Cultivating financial discipline involves making intentional decisions that align with financial goals. This includes responsible debt management, avoiding unnecessary spending and making informed spending decisions. The ability to delay gratification and prioritize long-term goals over short-term desires is a hallmark of financial discipline.

Adopting an entrepreneurial mindset can open new avenues to financial success. Identifying and seizing opportunities, adapting to change and fostering a spirit of innovation can lead to financial growth beyond traditional employment. Building multiple sources of income and exploring entrepreneurial activities contributes to financial resilience and independence.

Unlocking financial success is a dynamic and ongoing process that requires a combination of knowledge, planning, discipline and mindset. It is not just about accumulating wealth, but also involves making informed decisions that are in line with one's values and aspirations. By prioritizing financial literacy, strategic planning, disciplined saving, prudent investing, and adopting a growth mindset, individuals can navigate the complexities of personal finance and pave the way to lasting financial success.

I